D1517873

# EXTREMELY Weird ANIMALS

# NARWHAL

## BY CHRISTINA LEAF

BELLWETHER MEDIA • MINNEAPOLIS, MN

Jump into the cockpit and take flight with Pilot books. Your journey will take you on high-energy adventures as you learn about all that is wild, weird, fascinating, and fun!

This edition first published in 2014 by Bellwether Media, Inc.

No part of this publication may be reproduced in whole or in part without written permission of the publisher. For information regarding permission, write to Bellwether Media, Inc., Attention: Permissions Department, 5357 Penn Avenue South, Minneapolis, MN 55419.

Library of Congress Cataloging-in-Publication Data

Leaf, Christina, author.
  Narwhal / by Christina Leaf.
    pages cm. – (Pilot. Extremely Weird Animals)
  Summary: "Engaging images accompany information about narwhals. The combination of high-interest subject matter and narrative text is intended for students in grades 3 through 7"– Provided by publisher.
  Audience: Ages 7-12.
  Includes bibliographical references and index.
  ISBN 978-1-62617-075-9 (hardcover : alk. paper)
  1. Narwhal–Juvenile literature. I. Title.
  QL737.C433L43 2014
  599.5'43–dc23
                    2013036625

Printed in the United States of America, North Mankato, MN.

# TABLE OF CONTENTS

# A POD OF NARWHALS

It is a bright summer day off the northern coast of Canada. Despite the season, the air is cold. Far out in the sea, there are still chunks of ice floating in the water. Among the open spaces, dark gray shapes dip above and below the surface. Spurts of water shoot into the air. A pod of narwhals is in its summer home.

As they swim closer to shore, one narwhal pops its head out of the water. Its long, spiraled tusk pierces the air. Another narwhal appears and taps the tusk of the first with his own. The two engage for a moment in a brief tusking display. Then, both narwhals sink back under the water. Their smooth bodies soon disappear beneath the ice.

## Corpse Whale

In the Old Norse language, narwhal means "corpse whale." Sailors thought the animal's skin looked like a dead body!

# MARINE MAMMAL

The narwhal is a large marine mammal that swims in icy waters. This dark gray and white whale is closely related to the beluga. It is also a cousin of dolphins and porpoises. The narwhal is not as large as a blue or humpback whale, but it is still a big animal. It grows to be between 13 and 20 feet (4 and 6 meters) long. It can also weigh up to 3,500 pounds (1,587 kilograms).

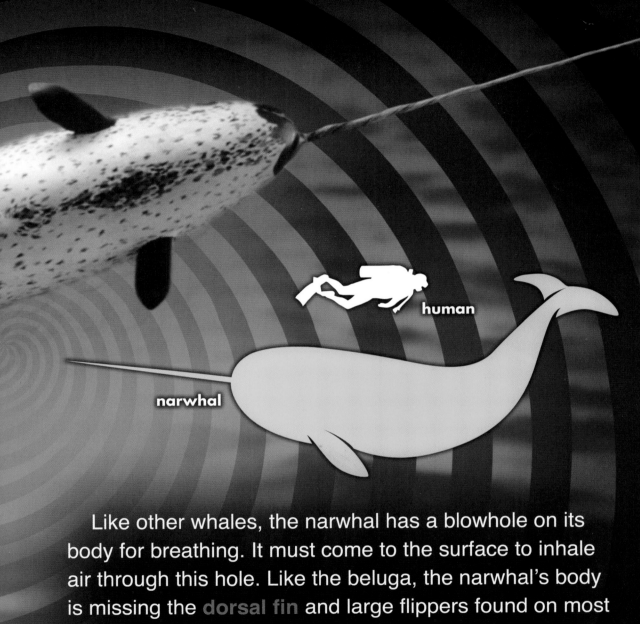

human

narwhal

Like other whales, the narwhal has a blowhole on its body for breathing. It must come to the surface to inhale air through this hole. Like the beluga, the narwhal's body is missing the **dorsal fin** and large flippers found on most other whales. Instead, it has only a small ridge on its back and two small fins on its sides. This is so it can swim just below ice chunks when searching for a breathing hole.

Most narwhals are found in the Arctic waters around northern Canada and eastern Greenland. A smaller number live in the waters north of Russia. The Arctic is a harsh climate. Animals that live there have to survive in extremely cold temperatures.

To stay warm, narwhals have a thick layer of blubber. This layer can be 3 to 4 inches (7.6 to 10 centimeters) thick. It acts like a blanket inside of their bodies. Their sausage-like shape also helps them trap in heat. This means the narwhal does not have to work as hard to stay warm.

narwhal range =

N
W    E
S

Narwhals migrate each year, too. They follow the Arctic ice pack. The movement of the ice pack is predictable. Traveling with it lowers the narwhals' chance of getting trapped.

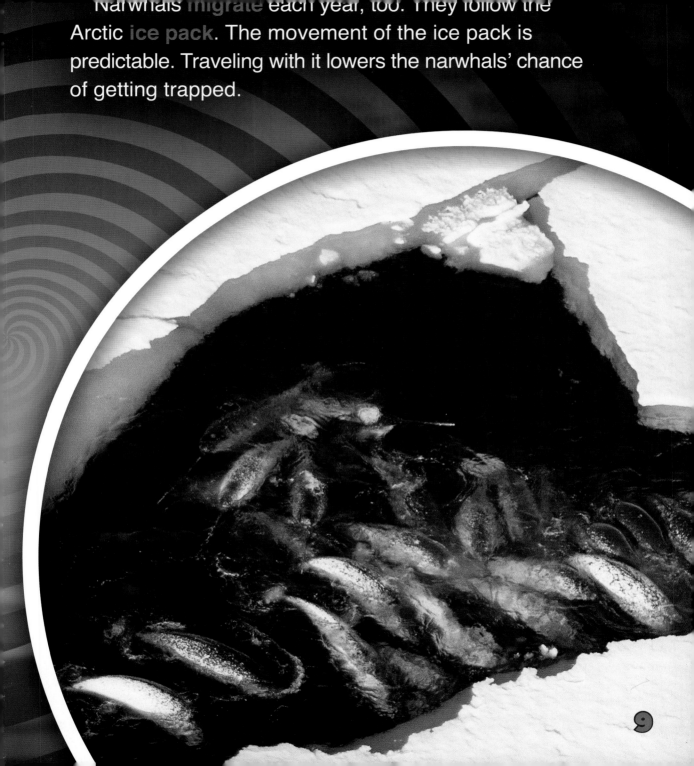

# A NOISY BUNCH

Narwhals are social animals. They often travel in pods of 10 to 15 narwhals. During long migrations, more than 1,000 narwhals might swim together! A pod of narwhals can be a noisy group. Narwhals use clicks and whistles to communicate with one another.

## HOW ECHOLOCATION WORKS

narwhal

prey

sound wave = [ ]   echo = [ ]

Narwhals also use these noises for echolocation. Their sounds bounce around underwater. When these noises hit something, they travel back to the narwhal. The animal uses these reflected sounds to figure out how far away food or a hole in the ice is. This helps the narwhal catch fish, squid, and shrimp for its meals. It also helps the animal find a place to come up for air.

**Going to Great Lengths**

Narwhals can dive more than a mile underwater to find food!

# UNICORN OF THE SEA

The narwhal is best known for the long horn that grows through its upper lip. This "horn" is actually a very long tusk, or tooth, made out of ivory. Usually only male narwhals have the famous tooth, but some females also develop one. A male's tusk can grow to be 9 feet (2.7 meters) long. Female tusks are typically much shorter. Narwhals also have a much smaller right tooth inside their upper lip. For most narwhals, this tooth does not grow long enough to be visible. In rare cases, this right tooth will also grow long. Then the narwhal has two tusks.

Other animals, such as walruses and elephants, have curved tusks. But the narwhal's is different. It is completely straight and made of swirls of ivory. This is why the narwhal has been nicknamed the "Unicorn of the Sea."

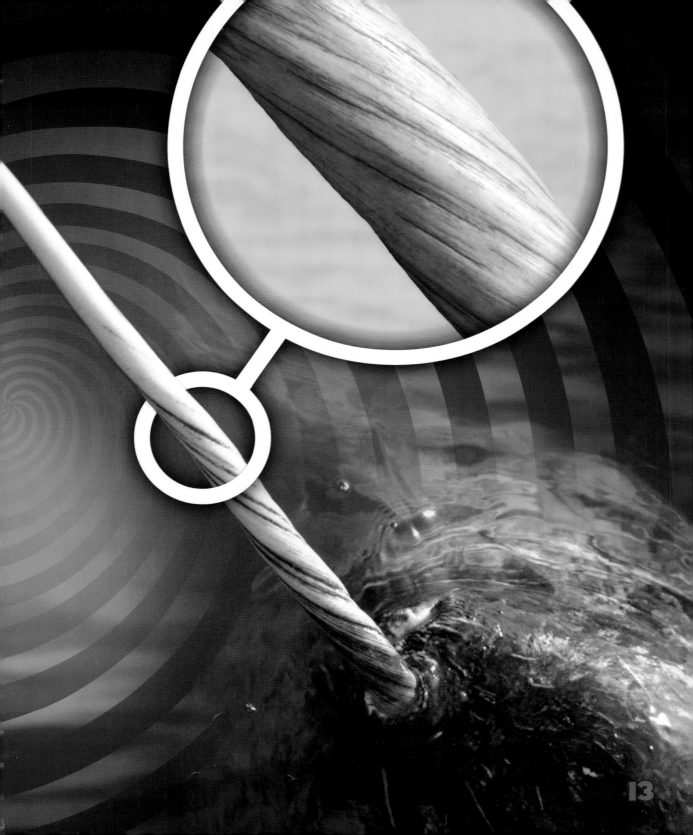

Narwhal tusks have fascinated people for centuries. Traders passed them off as unicorn horns, claiming they had magical powers. They were also prized by royalty. Kings and queens used them in their thrones and scepters. But no one was really sure what the narwhals used these tusks for.

Scientists have come up with a lot of theories about the narwhal tooth. Many have thought it was used in hunting. Some thought it was used for stabbing prey. However, research now shows that narwhals use other ways to catch their meals. In fact, sometimes their tusks might even get in the way. Other people thought that the tusks stirred up the ocean floor to uncover hiding animals. However, this would also interrupt their main method of finding food, echolocation.

**A Real Treasure**
Narwhal tusks were sold for more than ten times their weight in gold!

Despite the mysterious function of the tusk, scientists have known for a long time that it is a tooth. The narwhal's scientific name, *Monodon monoceros*, means "One tooth, one horn." So after careful research, a dentist came up with a new explanation. He claimed that the tooth was a way for the animals to learn about their surroundings.

Human teeth have a lot of nerves running through them. They can sense the temperature of a food or drink. A narwhal's tooth also has a lot of nerves. The dentist argued that this tooth could have a similar purpose. It may detect changes in temperature, pressure, salinity, and many other factors in the water. Researchers are still working to find out how narwhals use this information. One theory is that narwhals might sense when water is about to freeze. Then they can escape before they are trapped by the ice.

**Lots of Narwhals**

Many scientists agree that there are around 80,000 narwhals living in the wild.

The dentist's explanation for the narwhal's mysterious tusk is popular. But that does not mean that everyone believes it. Many biologists are still skeptical about this explanation. They argue that if the tusk is so important, all narwhals would have one instead of just males.

They offer a different explanation. Many say that the tooth is like a lion's mane. It is used to show off for female narwhals during mating. A longer tusk might show that a certain male is healthier than others. Tusking might also help show a female which male is best. Scientists are still trying to prove which theory is right. The only thing we know for sure is that we still have a lot to learn.

## Keeping Clean

Some people think that the male habit of tusking is just a way of brushing their tooth!

# ARCTIC SURVIVAL

Narwhals have a near threatened status. This means that although they are not in danger of dying out, they still need protection.

Thanks to protective laws, only native Inuit people are allowed to hunt narwhals. However, narwhals depend on a fragile environment. Human activities such as pollution are contributing to climate change, which is slowly melting the Arctic ice pack. As the water warms, the ice may become unpredictable in its movement. This can affect the narwhals' ability to find air holes.

Also, other Arctic creatures are food for narwhals. As the narwhals' environment disappears, so will their food. With such a delicate balance of life, humans have to be careful to protect these magical and mysterious Arctic animals.

EXTINCT

EXTINCT IN THE WILD

CRITICALLY ENDANGERED

ENDANGERED

VULNERABLE

NEAR THREATENED

LEAST CONCERN

# Narwhal Fact File

**Common Name:** narwhal

**Scientific Name:** Monodon monoceros

**Nickname:** Unicorn of the Sea

**Famous Feature:** long, spiraled tusk in males

**Distribution:** Arctic Ocean above North America, Arctic waters north of Russia

**Habitat:** deep, offshore Arctic waters

**Diet:** fish, squid, shrimp

**Life Span:** 50 years

**Current Status:** near threatened

# GLOSSARY

**Arctic**—the region around the north pole

**biologists**—scientists who study plant and animal life

**blubber**—the fat of whales and other large marine mammals

**climate change**—a long-lasting change in weather patterns; climate change is often traced to burning fossil fuels like oil and coal.

**dorsal fin**—the fin on the back of a fish, shark, or whale

**echolocation**—the process of using sound waves to find an object

**ice pack**—a large area of sea ice that has been crushed together; the Arctic ice pack covers the area around the north pole.

**marine mammal**—an animal that relies on the sea for food; marine mammals include dolphins, seals, whales, and walruses.

**migrate**—to travel from place to place, often with the seasons

**native**—originally from a specific place

**pod**—a group of whales

**pollution**—the act of harming an environment in a way that makes it unsafe for living

**salinity**—a measure of the amount of salt in seawater

**scepters**—batons carried by rulers to show authority

**skeptical**—questioning or doubting a claim

**theories**—ideas that are meant to explain facts or events

**tusking**—a behavior of male narwhals where they fight with their tusks; no one is sure why narwhals tusk.

# TO LEARN MORE

## AT THE LIBRARY

Marsico, Katie. *Narwhal*. Chicago, Ill.: Heinemann Library, 2012.

Miller, Sara Swan. *Whales of the Arctic*. New York, N.Y.: PowerKids Press, 2009.

Rake, Jody Sullivan. *Narwhal Whales Up Close*. Mankato, Minn.: Capstone Press, 2009.

## ON THE WEB

Learning more about narwhals is as easy as 1, 2, 3.

1. Go to www.factsurfer.com.

2. Enter "narwhals" into the search box.

3. Click the "Surf" button and you will see a list of related Web sites.

With factsurfer.com, finding more information is just a click away.

# INDEX

The images in this book are reproduced through the courtesy of: Paul Nicklen/ Getty Images, front cover, pp. 5, 14, 16-17, 18-19, 21; Flip Nicklin/ Getty Images, p. 9; Todd Mintz/ Alamy, p. 11; Bryan and Cherry Alexander/ Nature Picture Library, pp. 12-13; Interfoto/ Alamy, p. 13; Finaldream, p. 15; Africa Studio, p. 19.